ICKINSON
ted by TED HUGHES

D1638080

EMILY DICKINSON
Poems selected by TED HUGHES

faber and faber

First published in 1968
as *A Choice of Emily Dickinson's Verse*
by Faber and Faber Limited
3 Queen Square London WC1N 3AU

This edition first published in 2001

Photoset by Parker Typesetting Service, Leicester
Printed in Italy

A CIP record for this book
is available from the British Library
ISBN 0–571– 20735–9

10 9 8 7 6 5 4 3 2 1

Contents

Each poem in this list of contents is followed by two dates. The first date is the probable date of the earliest known manuscript; the second is the date of first publication.

Acknowledgements

The poems in this book are drawn from the complete poems of Emily Dickinson as edited by Thomas H. Johnson and published in a three-volume edition *The Poems of Emily Dickinson* (The Belknap Press of Harvard University Press) and in a one-volume edition *The Complete Poems of Emily Dickinson* (Little, Brown and Company). They are reprinted here by permission of the publishers and the Trustees of Amherst College from Thomas H. Johnson, Editor, *The Poems of Emily Dickinson*, Cambridge, Mass.: The Belknap Press of Harvard University Press, Copyright 1951, 1955, by The President and Fellows of Harvard College. And by permission of Houghton Mifflin Company from *Emily Dickinson Face to Face* by Martha Dickinson Bianchi, Copyright 1932, by Martha Dickinson Bianchi. And by permission of Little, Brown and Company from *The Complete Poems of Emily Dickinson* edited by Thomas H. Johnson, Copyright 1914, 1929, 1935, 1942, by Martha Dickinson Bianchi; Copyright © 1957, 1963, by Mary L. Hampson.

Introduction

Though she had a reputation among her friends for the occasional verses and poems which she enclosed in letters, Emily Dickinson's phenomenal secret output was unsuspected until after her death, in 1886, when her sister found the mass of manuscripts in her bureau. Some of it was neatly copied in her headlong, simplified script, and sewn loosely together in little booklets. The rest was in every possible state of mid-composition – a great problem for her editors, Mrs Mabel Loomis Todd and Millicent Todd Bingham, who prepared for the public eye successive selections of the poems, which came out between 1890 and 1945. Emily Dickinson's niece brought out other selections, so that by 1945 all the poems had been published, but in more or less heavily edited form. Apart from the frequent obscurity of Emily Dickinson's script and her habit of listing – at the crucial point in a poem – several alternative words or lines without clearly indicating which she finally preferred, the greatest problem for these editors was in reducing her punctuation of simple dashes to something more orthodox. They acted boldly, but not to everybody's satisfaction. The subsequent experiments in this line by such sensitive and sympathetic critics as John Crowe Ransom have not checked the growing opinion that Emily Dickinson's eccentric dashes are an integral part of her method and style, and cannot be translated to commas, semicolons and the rest without deadening the wonderfully naked voltage of the poems.

Accordingly, T. H. Johnson re-edited the *Complete Poems*, in a variorum edition, retaining everything – as closely as possible – just as the poet left it. And so in 1955 Emily Dickinson's poetry appeared for the first time without editorial adjustments, and complete. In 1960, T. H. Johnson made an edition for the ordinary reader in which he reduced the manuscript variants of the poems to a single text of each, again following the poet's directives as far as he could determine them, a feat of taste and tact to which this present selection is indebted. On the final count, the collected poems number 1775. Emily Dickinson only ever saw six of these in print, and then they had been so heavily corrected, by editorial hands, to the taste of the day, that she seems to have resigned herself after that to posterity or nothing.

She is one of the oddest and most intriguing personalities in literary history. She was born in 1830, in Amherst, Massachusetts. As a girl she was notorious for her comic wit and high-spirited originality, among her friends and within her family. But she showed little inclination to venture into the world, and less and less as time went on. Even at twenty-four she was saying, 'I don't go from home, unless emergency leads me by the hand.' Eventually, and by degrees, she developed this into nearly complete self-imprisonment in her father's house, avoiding all visitors. Her father was a leading citizen of the small town, a popular lawyer, active in local affairs, political and social, with a wide circle of friends, some of whom had a notable part in the public life of the state. To Emily in particular he appeared as a stern, awe-inspiring man. 'His heart was pure and terrible and I think no other like it exists,' she wrote later, but he had a large library, and it was perhaps through his concerns and acquaintances that his intense daughter eavesdropped on the world.

When she did meet visitors, she gave no impression of a person timid or withdrawn. One T. W. Higginson, to whom she had written asking for criticism of her poems, visited her in 1870, and though their long correspondence had prepared him for something unusual he was astounded and over-whelmed by the barrage of extravagant intensities and imagery and epigrams that met him. He afterwards described the conversation of his 'half-cracked poetess' as 'the very wantonness of overstatement' and said 'I was never with anyone who drained my nerve power so much.' She made no attempt to conceal her ecstatic delight in life. 'My Business is to love . . . my Business is to sing,' and 'I find ecstasy in living . . . the mere sense of living is joy enough.' One can imagine how her retreat from the world must have stepped this temperament up to terrific pressure, till any excitement at all became explosive. 'Friday I tasted life. It was a vast morsel. A circus passed the house – still I feel the red in my mind.' It was to Higginson that she described herself as 'small, like the Wren, and my hair is bold, like the Chestnut bur – and my eyes, like the Sherry in the Glass, that the Guest leaves.' In her poems she presents herself as 'freckled' and 'Gypsy'.

Around 1860, something decisive happened to Emily Dickinson. How far it was the natural point of maturation of many things in herself, and how much it was triggered by some outer event, is not known, though the possibilities have been endlessly discussed. But the effect was a conflagration within her that produced just about one thousand poems in six years, more than half her total. In 1862 alone it has been calculated that she wrote 366 poems. Those years coincided with the national agitations of the Civil War, with her own coming to mental maturity, and with the beginning of her thirties – when perhaps she realized that her unusual endowment of love was not going to be asked for. But the central themes of the poems have suggested to many readers that the key event was a great and final disappointment in her love for some particular person, about this time. There are two or three likely candidates for the role, and some evidence in letters. This theory supposes that the eruption of her imagination and poetry followed when she shifted her passion, with the energy of desperation, from this lost person onto his only possible substitute – the entire Universe in its Divine aspect. She certainly describes this operation in her poems several times, and it's hard not to believe that something of the sort happened. Therefore, the marriage that had been denied in the real world, went forward in the spiritual – on her side – as dozens of her poems witness:

Title divine – is Mine!
The Wife – without the Sign!

The forces which now came together in the crucible of her imagination decided her greatness. One of the most weighty circumstances, and the most interesting, was that just as the Universe in its Divine aspect became the mirror-image of her 'husband', so the whole religious dilemma of New England, at that most critical moment in its history, became the mirror-image of her relationship to him – of her 'marriage', in fact. And so her spiritualized love and its difficulties became also a topical religious disputation on the grandest scale.

At that time, the old Calvinism of the New England states was in open battle against the spirit of the new age – the Higher Criticism that was dissolving the Bible, the broadening, liberalizing influence of Transcendentalism, the general scientific scepticism which, in America, was doubly rabid under the backlash of the ruthless, selective pragmatism of the frontier and the international-scale hatreds smuggled in by the freedom-grabbers. On the one hand, radical Puritan revivals were sweeping Emily Dickinson's friends and relatives away from the flesh and the world, like epidemics which she was almost alone among her friends in resisting, and on the other hand Jonathan Edwards announced that the visible Universe was 'an emanation of God for the pure joy of Creation in which the creatures find their justification by yielding assent to the beauty of the whole, even though it slay them.' Beyond this, the Civil War was melting down the whole nation in an ideological gamble of total suicide or renewal in unity. The Indian tribes and the great sea of buffalo waited on the virgin plains, while Darwin wrote his chapters. The powers that struggled for reconciliation in Emily Dickinson were no less than those which were unmaking and remaking America.

In all this, as her poems testify, she kept her head. Whether the divine 'You', to which her poems are regularly addressed, be a Pan/Christ or the absconded Rev. Charles Wadsworth, a Jehovah/Nature or the inaccessible Mr Otis P. Lord, Judge of the Supreme Court of Massachusetts, or an altogether darker enigma, it is impossible to tell, but whichever it was, they had a difficult spiritual 'wife' in her. She was devoted, she led the life of a recluse and she wore white, proper for a bride of the spirit, and she daily composed poems that read like devotions. But she was first of all true to herself and her wits. Whether from Church or Science, she would accept nothing by hearsay or on authority, though she was tempted every way. She reserved herself in some final suspension of judgement. So her poems record not only her ecstatic devotion, but her sharp, sceptical independence, her doubt, and what repeatedly opens under her ecstasy – her despair.

However important for her poetry her life of love, with all its difficulties, may have been, there is another experience, quite as important, which seems to have befallen her often, and which had nothing to do with her outer life. It is the subject of some of her greatest poems, and all her best poems touch on it. It is what throws the characteristic aura of immensity and chill over her ideas and images. She never seems to have known quite what to think of it. It seems to have recurred to her as a physical state, almost a trance state. In this condition, there opened to her a vision – final reality, her own soul, the soul within the Universe – in all her descriptions of its nature, she never presumed to give it a name. It was her deeper, holiest experience; it was also the most terrible: timeless, deathly, vast, intense. It was like a contradiction to everything that the life in her trusted and loved, it was almost a final revelation of horrible Nothingness –

Most – like Chaos – stopless – cool
Without a chance – or spar –
Or even a Report of Land
To justify Despair

– and as such, it was the source of the paradox which is her poetic self, and which proliferates throughout her feelings, her ideas, her language, her imagery, her verse technique, in all kinds of ways. At any moment she is likely to feel it ushering itself in, with electrical storms, exalted glimpses of objects, eerie openings of the cosmos –

A wind that rose, though not a leaf
In any forest stirred –

Remaining true to this, she could make up her mind about nothing. It stared through her life. Registering everywhere and in everything the icy chill of its nearness, she did not know what to think. The one thing she was sure about, was that it was there, and that its speech was poetry. In its light, all other concerns floated free of finality, became merely relative, susceptible to her artistic play. It was a mystery, and there was only one thing she relied on to solve it, and that was death. Death obsessed her, as the one act that could take her the one necessary step beyond her vision. Death would carry her and her sagacity clean through the riddle. She deferred all her questions to death's solution. And so these three – whatever it was that lay beyond her frightening vision, and the crowded, beloved Creation around her, and Death – became her Holy Trinity. What she divined of their Holiness was what she could divine of their poetry. And it is in her devotion to this Trinity, rather than in anything to do with the more orthodox terminology which she used so freely and familiarly, that she became 'the greatest religious poet America has produced'.

In a way, it was the precision of her feeling for language, which is one department of honesty, that kept her to the painful shortcoming of her suspended judgement, and saved her from the easy further step of abstraction into philosophy and shared religion. And it is in her verbal genius that all her gifts and convulsive sufferings came to focus. She was able to manage such a vast subject matter, and make it so important to us, purely because of the strength and ingenuities of her poetic style.

There is the slow, small metre, a device for bringing each syllable into close-up, as under a microscope; there is the deep steady focus, where all the words lie in precise and yet somehow free relationships, so that the individual syllables seem to be on the point of slipping into utterly new meanings, all pressing to be uncovered; there is the mosaic, pictogram concentration of ideas into which she codes a volcanic elemental imagination, an apocalyptic vision; there is the tranced suspense and deliberation in her punctuation of dashes, and the riddling, oblique artistic strategies, the Shakespearian texture of the language, solid with metaphor, saturated with the homeliest imagery and experience; the freakish blood-and-nerve paradoxical vitality of her Latinisms; the musical games – of opposites, parallels, mirrors, Chinese puzzles, harmonizing and counterpointing whole worlds of reference; and everywhere there is the teeming carnival of world-life. It is difficult to exhaust the unique art and pleasures of her poetic talent. With the hymn and the riddle, those two small domestic implements, she grasped the 'centre' and the 'circumference' of things – to use two of her favourite expressions – as surely as human imagination ever has.

To select the poems in this volume has not been easy. Her unique and inspired pieces are very many, and very varied. In the limits of this 'selection' it was not possible to be representative. Finally, I chose the pieces I liked best at the time of choosing, well aware that among so many poems of such strong charm this choice must be far from final, for me or for any reader.

Ted Hughes

EMILY DICKINSON

That Love is all there is,
Is all we know of Love;
It is enough, the freight should be
Proportioned to the groove.

*

Exultation is the going
Of an inland soul to sea,
Past the houses – past the headlands –
Into deep Eternity –

Bred as we, among the mountains,
Can the sailor understand
The divine intoxication
Of the first league out from land?

*

I have never seen 'Volcanoes' –
But, when Travellers tell
How those old – phlegmatic mountains
Usually so still –

Bear within – appalling Ordnance,
Fire, and smoke, and gun,
Taking Villages for breakfast,
And appalling Men –

If the stillness is Volcanic
In the human face
When upon a pain Titanic
Features keep their place –

If at length the smouldering anguish
Will not overcome –
And the palpitating Vineyard
In the dust, be thrown?

If some loving Antiquary,
On Resumption Morn,
Will not cry with joy 'Pompeii'!
To the Hills return!

*

An awful Tempest mashed the air –
The clouds were gaunt, and few –
A Black – as of a Spectre's Cloak
Hid Heaven and Earth from view.

The creatures chuckled on the Roofs –
And whistled in the air –
And shook their fists –
And gnashed their teeth –
And swung their frenzied hair.

The morning lit – the Birds arose –
The Monster's faded eyes
Turned slowly to his native coast –
And peace – was Paradise!

*

It's such a little thing to weep –
So short a thing to sigh –
And yet – by Trades – the size of *these*
We men and women die!

*

4

Safe in their Alabaster Chambers –
Untouched by Morning –
And untouched by Noon –
Lie the meek members of the Resurrection –
Rafter of Satin – and Roof of Stone!

Grand go the Years – in the Crescent – above them –
Worlds scoop their Arcs –
And Firmaments – row –
Diadems – drop – and Doges – surrender –
Soundless as dots – on a Disc of Snow –

*

There's a certain Slant of light,
Winter Afternoons –
That oppresses, like the Heft
Of Cathedral Tunes –

Heavenly Hurt, it gives us –
We can find no scar,
But internal difference,
Where the Meanings, are –

None may teach it – Any –
'Tis the Seal Despair –
An imperial affliction
Sent us of the Air –

When it comes, the Landscape listens –
Shadows – hold their breath –
When it goes, 'tis like the Distance
On the look of Death –

*

I felt a Funeral, in my Brain,
And Mourners to and fro
Kept treading – treading – till it seemed
That Sense was breaking through –

And when they all were seated,
A Service, like a Drum –
Kept beating – beating – till I thought
My Mind was going numb –

And then I heard them lift a Box
And creak across my Soul
With those same Boots of Lead, again,
Then space – began to toll,

And all the Heavens were a Bell,
And Being, but an Ear,
And I, and Silence, some strange Race
Wrecked, solitary here –

And then a Plank in Reason, broke,
And I dropped down, and down –
And hit a World, at every plunge,
And Finished knowing – then –

*

That after Horror – that 'twas *us*
That passed the mouldering Pier –
Just as the Granite Crumb let go –
Our Savior, by a Hair –

A second more, had dropped too deep
For Fisherman to plumb –
The very profile of the Thought
Puts Recollection numb –

The possibility – to pass
Without a Moment's Bell –
Into Conjecture's presence –
Is like a Face of Steel –
That suddenly looks into ours
With a metallic grin –
The Cordiality of Death –
Who drills his Welcome in –

*

A Clock stopped –
Not the Mantel's –
Geneva's farthest skill
Can't put the puppet bowing –
That just now dangled still –

An awe came on the Trinket!
The Figures hunched, with pain –
Then quivered out of Decimals –
Into Degreeless Noon –

It will not stir for Doctors –
The Pendulum of snow –
This Shopman importunes it –
While cool – concernless No –

Nods from the Gilded pointers –
Nods from the Seconds slim –
Decades of Arrogance between
The Dial life –
And Him –

*

How the old Mountains drip with Sunset
How the Hemlocks burn –
How the Dun Brake is draped in Cinder
By the Wizard Sun –

How the old Steeples hand the Scarlet
Till the Ball is full –
Have I the lip of the Flamingo
That I dare to tell?

Then, how the Fire ebbs like Billows –
Touching all the Grass
With a departing – Sapphire – feature –
As a Duchess passed –

How a small Dusk crawls on the Village
Till the Houses blot
And the odd Flambeau, no men carry
Glimmer on the Street –

How it is Night – in Nest and Kennel –
And where was the Wood –
Just a Dome of Abyss is Bowing
Into Solitude –

These are the Visions flitted Guido –
Titian – never told –
Domenichino dropped his pencil –
Paralyzed, with Gold –

*

The Soul selects her own Society –
Then – shuts the Door –
To her divine Majority –
Present no more –

Unmoved – she notes the Chariots – pausing
At her low Gate –
Unmoved – an Emperor be kneeling
Upon her Mat –

I've known her – from an ample nation –
Choose One –
Then – close the Valves of her attention –
Like Stone –

*

The Murmur of a Bee
A Witchcraft – yieldeth me –
If any ask me why –
'Twere easier to die –
Than tell –

The Red upon the Hill
Taketh away my will –
If anybody sneer –
Take care – for God is here –
That's all.

The Breaking of the Day
Addeth to my Degree –
If any ask me how –
Artist – who drew me so –
Must tell!

*

The Mushroom is the Elf of Plants –
At Evening, it is not –
At morning, in a Truffled Hut
It stop upon a Spot

As if it tarried always
And yet its whole Career
Is shorter than a Snake's Delay
And fleeter than a Tare –

'Tis Vegetation's Juggler –
The Germ of Alibi –
Doth like a Bubble antedate
And like a Bubble, hie –

I feel as if the Grass was pleased
To have it intermit –
This surreptitious scion
Of Summer's circumspect.

Had Nature any supple Face
Or could she one contemn –
Had Nature an Apostate –
That Mushroom – it is Him!

*

He fumbles at your Soul
As Players at the Keys
Before they drop full Music on –
He stuns you by degrees –
Prepares your brittle Nature
For the Ethereal Blow
By fainter Hammers – further heard –
Then nearer – Then so slow
Your breath has time to straighten –
Your Brain – to bubble Cool –
Deals – One – imperial – Thunderbolt –
That scalps your naked Soul –
When Winds take Forests in their Paws –
The Universe – is still –

*

I'll tell you how the Sun rose –
A Ribbon at a time –
The Steeples swam in Amethyst –
The news, like Squirrels, ran –
The Hills untied their Bonnets –
The Bobolinks – begun –
Then I said softly to myself –
'That must have been the Sun'!
But how he set – I know not –
There seemed a purple stile
That little Yellow boys and girls
Were climbing all the while –
Till when they reached the other side,
A Dominie in Gray –
Put gently up the evening Bars –
And led the flock away –

*

After great pain, a formal feeling comes –
The Nerves sit ceremonious, like Tombs –
The stiff Heart questions was it He, that bore,
And Yesterday, or Centuries before?

The Feet, mechanical, go round –
Of Ground, or Air, or Ought –
A Wooden way
Regardless grown,
A Quartz contentment, like a stone –

This is the Hour of Lead –
Remembered, if outlived,
As Freezing persons, recollect the Snow –
First – Chill – then Stupor – then the letting go

*

I dreaded that first Robin, so,
But He is mastered, now,
I'm some accustomed to Him grown,
He hurts a little, though –

I thought if I could only live
Till that first Shout got by –
Not all Pianos in the Woods
Had power to mangle me –

I dared not meet the Daffodils –
For fear their Yellow Gown
Would pierce me with a fashion
So foreign to my own –

I wished the Grass would hurry –
So – when 'twas time to see –
He'd be too tall, the tallest one
Could stretch – to look at me –

I could not bear the Bees should come,
I wished they'd stay away
In those dim countries where they go,
What word had they, for me?

They're here, though; not a creature failed –
No blossom stayed away
In gentle deference to me –
The Queen of Calvary –

Each one salutes me, as he goes,
And I, my childish Plumes,
Lift, in bereaved acknowledgment
Of their unthinking Drums –

*

I went to Heaven –
'Twas a small Town –
Lit – with a Ruby –
Lathed – with Down –

Stiller – than the fields
At the full Dew –
Beautiful – as Pictures –
No Man drew.
People –like the Moth –
Of Mechlin – frames –
Duties – of Gossamer –
And Eider – names –
Almost – contented –
I – could be –

'Mong such unique
Society –

*

I saw no Way – The Heavens were stitched –
I felt the Columns close –
The Earth reversed her Hemispheres –
I touched the Universe –

And back it slid – and I alone –
A Speck upon a Ball –
Went out upon Circumference –
Beyond the Dip of Bell –

*

'Twas like a Maelstrom, with a notch,
That nearer, every Day,
Kept narrowing its boiling Wheel
Until the Agony

Toyed coolly with the final inch
Of your delirious Hem –
And you dropt, lost,
When something broke –
And let you from a Dream –

As if a Goblin with a Gauge –
Kept measuring the Hours –
Until you felt your Second
Weigh, helpless, in his Paws –

And not a Sinew – stirred – could help,
And sense was setting numb –
When God – remembered – and the Fiend
Let go, then, Overcome –

As if your Sentence stood – pronounced –
And you were frozen led
From Dungeon's luxury of Doubt
To Gibbets, and the Dead –

And when the Film had stitched your eyes
A Creature gasped 'Reprieve'!
Which Anguish was the utterest – then –
To perish, or to live?

*

If What we could – were what we would –
Criterion – be small –
It is the Ultimate of Talk –
The impotence to Tell –

*

The Month have ends – the Years – a knot –
No Power can untie
To stretch a little further
A Skein of Misery –

The Earth lays back these tired lives
In her mysterious Drawers –
Too tenderly, that any doubt
An ultimate Repose –

The manner of the Children –
Who weary of the Day –
Themself – the noisy Plaything
They cannot put away –

*

The Wind – tapped like a tired Man –
And like a Host – 'Come in'
I boldly answered – entered then
My Residence within

A Rapid – footless Guest –
To offer whom a Chair
Were as impossible as hand
A Sofa to the Air –

No Bone had He to bind Him –
His Speech was like the Push
Of numerous Humming Birds at once
From a superior Bush –

His Countenance – a Billow –
His Fingers, as He passed
Let go a music – as of tunes
Blown tremulous in Glass –

He visited – still flitting –
Then like a timid Man
Again, He tapped – 'twas flurriedly –
And I became alone –

*

Sweet – safe – Houses –
Glad – gay – Houses –
Sealed so stately tight –
Lids of Steel – on Lids of Marble –
Locking Bare feet out –

Brooks of Plush – in Banks of Satin
Not so softly fall
As the laughter – and the whisper –
From their People Pearl –

No Bald Death – affront their Parlors –
No Bold Sickness come
To deface their Stately Treasures –
Anguish – and the Tomb –

Hum by – in Muffled Coaches –
Lest they – wonder Why –
Any – for the Press of Smiling –
Interrupt – to die –

*

I died for Beauty – but was scarce
Adjusted in the Tomb
When One who died for Truth, was lain
In an adjoining Room –

He questioned softly 'Why I failed'?
'For Beauty', I replied –
'And I – for Truth – Themself are One –
We Brethren, are', He said –

And so, as Kinsmen, met a Night –
We talked between the Rooms –
Until the Moss had reached our lips
and covered up – our names –

*

I heard a Fly buzz – when I died –
The Stillness in the Room
Was like the Stillness in the Air –
Between the Heaves of Storm –

The Eyes around – had wrung them dry –
And Breaths were gathering firm
For that last Onset – when the King
Be witnessed – in the Room –

I willed my Keepsakes – Signed away
What portion of me be
Assignable – and then it was
There interposed a Fly –

With Blue – uncertain stumbling Buzz –
Between the light – and me –
And then the Windows failed – and then
I could not see to see –

*

The Red – Blaze – is the Morning –
The Violet – is Noon –
The Yellow – Day – is falling –
And after that – is none –

17

But Miles of Sparks – at Evening –
Reveal the Width that burned –
The Territory Argent – that
Never yet – consumed –

*

A Solemn thing within the Soul
To feel itself get ripe –
And golden hang – while farther up –
The Maker's Ladders stop –
And in the Orchard far below –
You hear a Being – drop –

A Wonderful – to feel the Sun
Still toiling at the Cheek
You thought was finished –
Cool of eye, and critical of Work –
He shifts the stem – a little –
To give your Core – a look –

But solemnest – to know
Your chance in Harvest moves
A little nearer – Every Sun
The Single – to some lives.

*

Civilization – spurns – the Leopard!
Was the Leopard – bold?
Deserts – never rebuked her Satin –
Ethiop – her Gold –
Tawny – her Customs –
She was Conscious –
Spotted – her Dun Gown –
This was the Leopard's nature – Signor –
Need – a keeper – frown?

Pity – the Pard – that left her Asia –
Memories – of Palm –
Cannot be stifled – with Narcotic –
Nor suppressed – with Balm

*

This World is not Conclusion.
A Species stands beyond –
Invisible, as Music –
But positive, as Sound –
It beckons, and it baffles –
Philosophy – don't know –
And through a Riddle, at the last –
Sagacity, must go –
To guess it, puzzles scholars –
To gain it, Men have borne
Contempt of Generations
And Crucifixion, shown –
Faith slips – and laughs, and rallies –
Blushes, if any see –
Plucks at a twig of Evidence –
And asks a Vane, the way –
Much Gesture, from the Pulpit –
Strong Hallelujahs roll –
Narcotics cannot still the Tooth
That nibbles at the soul –

*

It was not Death, for I stood up,
And all the Dead, lie down –
It was not Night, for all the Bells
Put out their Tongues, for Noon.

It was not Frost, for on my Flesh
I felt Siroccos – crawl –
Not Fire – for just my Marble feet
Could keep a Chancel, cool –

And yet, it tasted, like them all,
The Figures I have seen
Set orderly, for Burial,
Reminded me, of mine –

As if my life were shaven,
And fitted to a frame,
And could not breathe without a key,
And 'twas like Midnight, some –

When everything that ticked – has stopped –
And space stares all around –
Or Grisly frosts – first Autumn morns,
Repeal the Beating Ground –

But, most, like Chaos – Stopless – cool –
Without a Chance, or Spar –
Or even a Report of Land –
To justify – Despair.

*

The Soul has Bandaged moments –
When too appalled to stir –
She feels some ghastly Fright come up
And stop to look at her –

Salute her – with long fingers –
Caress her freezing hair –
Sip, Goblin, from the very lips
The Lover – hovered – o'er –
Unworthy, that a thought so mean
Accost a Theme – so – fair –

The soul has moments of Escape –
When bursting all the doors –
She dances like a Bomb, abroad,
And swings upon the Hours,

As do the Bee – delirious borne –
Long Dungeoned from his Rose –
Touch Liberty – then know no more,
But Noon, and Paradise –

The Soul's retaken moments –
When, Felon led along,
With shackles on the plumed feet,
And staples, in the Song,

The Horror welcomes her, again,
These, are not brayed of Tongue –

*

Departed – to the Judgment –
A Mighty Afternoon –
Great Clouds – like Ushers – leaning –
Creation – looking on –

The Flesh – Surrendered – Cancelled –
The Bodiless – begun –
Two Worlds – like Audiences – disperse –
And leave the Soul – alone –

*

I think the Hemlock likes to stand
Upon the Marge of Snow –
It suits his own Austerity –
And satisfies an awe.

That men, must slake in Wilderness –
And in the Desert – cloy –
An instinct for the Hoar, the Bald –
Lapland's – necessity –

The Hemlock's nature thrives – on cold –
The Gnash of Northern winds
Is sweetest nutriment – to him –
His best Norwegian Wines –

To satin Races – he is nought –
But Children on the Don,
Beneath his Tabernacles, play,
And Dnieper Wrestlers, run.

*

I tried to think a lonelier Thing
Than any I had seen –
Some Polar Expiation – An Omen in the Bone
Of Death's tremendous nearness –

I probed Retrieveless things
My Duplicate – to borrow –
A Haggard Comfort springs

From the belief that Somewhere –
Within the Clutch of Thought –
There dwells one other Creature
Of Heavenly Love – forgot –

I plucked at our Partition
As One should pry the Walls –
Between Himself – and Horror's Twin –
Within Opposing Cells –

I almost strove to clasp his Hand,
Such Luxury – it grew –
That as Myself – could pity Him –
Perhaps he – pitied me –

*

The Heart asks Pleasure – first
And then – Excuse from Pain –
And then – those little Anodynes
That deaden suffering –

And then – to go to sleep –
And then – if it should be
The will of its Inquisitor
The privilege to die –

*

I fear a Man of frugal Speech –
I fear a Silent Man –
Haranguer – I can overtake –
Or Babbler – entertain –

But He who weigheth – While the Rest
Expend their furthest pound –
Of this Man – I am wary –
I fear that He is Grand –

*

One Crucifixion is recorded – only –
How many be
Is not affirmed of Mathematics –
Or History –

One Calvary – exhibited to Stranger –
As many be
As persons – or Peninsulas –
Gethsemane –

Is but a Province – in the Being's Centre –
Judea –
For Journey – or Crusade's Achieving –
Too near –

Our Lord – indeed – made Compound Witness –
And Yet –
There's newer – nearer Crucifixion
Than That –

*

The Brain, within its Groove
Runs evenly – and true –
But let a Splinter swerve –
'Twere easier for You –

To put a Current back –
When Floods have slit the Hills –
And scooped a Turnpike for Themselves –
And trodden out the Mills –

*

It knew no lapse, nor Diminution –
But large – serene –
Burned on – until through Dissolution –
It failed from Men –

I could not deem these Planetary forces
Annulled –
But suffered an Exchange of Territory –
Or World –

*

There is a pain – so utter –
It swallows substance up –
Then covers the Abyss with Trance –
So Memory can step
Around – across – upon it –
As one within a Swoon –
Goes safely – where an open eye –
Would drop Him – Bone by Bone.

*

A still – Volcano – Life –
That flickered in the night –
When it was dark enough to do
Without erasing sight –

A quiet – Earthquake Style –
Too subtle to suspect
By natures this side Naples –
The North cannot detect

The Solemn – Torrid – Symbol –
The lips that never lie –
Whose hissing Corals part – and shut
And Cities – ooze away –

*

The Brain – is wider than the Sky –
For – put them side by side –
The one the other will contain
With ease – and You – beside –

The Brain is deeper than the sea –
For – hold them – Blue to Blue –
The one the other will absorb –
As Sponges – Buckets – do –

The Brain is just the weight of God –
For – Heft them – Pound for Pound –
And they will differ – if they do –
As Syllable from Sound –

*

One need not be a Chamber – to be Haunted –
One need not be a House –
The Brain has Corridors – surpassing
Material Place –

Far safer, of a Midnight Meeting
External Ghost
Than its interior Confronting –
That Cooler Host.

Far safer, through an Abbey gallop,
The Stones a'chase –
Than Unarmed, one's a'self encounter –
In lonesome Place –

Ourself behind ourself, concealed –
Should startle most –
Assassin hid in our Apartment
Be Horror's least.

The Body – borrows a Revolver –
He bolts the Door –
O'erlooking a superior spectre –
Or More –

*

The Soul that hath a Guest
Doth seldom go abroad –
Diviner Crowd at Home –
Obliterate the need –

And Courtesy forbid
A Host's departure when
Upon Himself be visiting
The Emperor of Men –

*

I'll send the feather from my Hat!
Who knows – but at the sight of *that*
My Sovereign will relent?
As trinket – worn by faded Child –
Confronting eyes long – comforted –
Blisters the Adamant!

*

'*Speech*' – is a prank of *Parliament* –
'*Tears*' – a trick of the *nerve* –
But the Heart with the heaviest freight on –
Doesn't – always – move –

*

Victory comes late –
And is held low to freezing lips –
Too rapt with frost
To take it –
How sweet it would have tasted –
Just a Drop –
Was God so economical?
His Table's spread too high for Us –
Unless We dine on tiptoe –
Crumbs – fit such little mouths –
Cherries – suit Robins –
The Eagle's Golden Breakfast strangles – Them
God keep His Oath to Sparrows –
Who of little Love – know how to starve –

*

I sometimes drop it, for a Quick –
The Thought to be alive –
Anonymous Delight to know –
And madder – to conceive –

Consoles a Woe so monstrous
That did it tear all Day,
Without an instant's Respite –
'Twould look too far – to Die –

Delirium – diverts the Wretch
For Whom the Scaffold neighs –
The Hammock's Motion lulls the Heads
So close on Paradise –

A Reef – crawled easy from the Sea
Eats off the Brittle Line –
The Sailor doesn't know the Stroke –
Until He's past the Pain –

*

Because I could not stop for Death –
He kindly stopped for me –
The Carriage held but just Ourselves –
And Immortality.

We slowly drove – He knew no haste
And I had put away
My labor and my leisure too,
For His Civility –

We passed the School, where Children strove
At Recess – in the Ring –
We passed the Fields of Gazing Grain –
We passed the Setting Sun –

Or rather – He passed Us –
The Dews drew quivering and chill –
For only Gossamer, my Gown –
My Tippet – only Tulle –

We paused before a House that seemed
A Swelling of the Ground –
The Roof was scarcely visible –
The Cornice – in the Ground –

Since then –'tis Centuries – and yet
Feels shorter than the Day
I first surmised the Horses' Heads
Were toward Eternity –

*

Four Trees – upon a solitary Acre –
Without Design
Or Order, or Apparent Action –
Maintain –

The Sun – upon a Morning meets them –
The Wind –
No nearer Neighbor – have they –
But God –

The Acre gives them – Place –
They – Him – Attention of Passer by –
Of Shadow, or of Squirrel, haply –
Or Boy –

What Deed is Theirs unto the General Nature –
What Plan
They severally – retard – or further –
Unknown –

*

Bloom upon the Mountain – stated –
Blameless of a Name –
Efflorescence of a Sunset –
Reproduced – the same –

Seed, had I, my Purple Sowing
Should endow the Day –
Not a Tropic of a Twilight –
Show itself away –

Who for tilling – to the Mountain
Come, and disappear –
Whose be Her Renown, or fading,
Witness, is not here –

While I state – the Solemn Petals,
Far as North – and East,
Far as South and West – expanding –
Culminate – in Rest –

And the Mountain to the Evening
Fit His Countenance –
Indicating, by no Muscle –
The Experience –

*

My Soul – accused me – And I quailed –
As Tongues of Diamond had reviled
All else accused me – and I smiled –
My Soul – that Morning – was My friend –

Her favor – is the best Disdain
Toward Artifice of Time – or Men –
But her Disdain – 'twere lighter bear
A finger of Enamelled Fire –

*

My Life had stood – a Loaded Gun –
In Corners – till a Day
The Owner passed – identified –
And carried Me away –

And now We roam in Sovereign Woods –
And now We hunt the Doe –
And every time I speak for Him –
The Mountains straight reply –

And do I smile, such cordial light
Upon the Valley glow –
It is as a Vesuvian face
Had let its pleasure through –

And when at Night – Our good Day done –
I guard My Master's Head –
'Tis better than the Eider-Duck's
Deep Pillow – to have shared –

To foe of His – I'm deadly foe –
None stir the second time –
On whom I lay a Yellow Eye –
Or an emphatic Thumb –

Though I than He – may longer live
He longer must – than I –
For I have but the power to kill,
Without – the power to die –

*

Presentiment – is that long Shadow – on the Lawn –
Indicative that Suns go down –

The Notice to the startled Grass
That Darkness – is about to pass –

*

The Loneliness One dare not sound –
And would as soon surmise
As in its Grave go plumbing
To ascertain the size –

The Loneliness whose worst alarm
Is lest itself should see –
And perish from before itself
For just a scrutiny –

The Horror not to be surveyed –
But skirted in the Dark –
With Consciousness suspended –
And Being under Lock –

I fear me this – is Loneliness –
The Maker of the soul
Its Caverns and its Corridors
Illuminate – or seal –

*

Through the strait pass of suffering –
The Martyrs – even – trod.
Their feet – upon Temptation –
Their faces – upon God –

A stately – shriven – Company –
Convulsion – playing round –
Harmless – as streaks of Meteor –
Upon a Planet's Bond –

Their faith – the everlasting troth –
Their Expectation – fair –

The Needle – to the North Degree –
Wades – so – thro' polar Air!

*

When One has given up One's life
The parting with the rest
Feels easy, as when Day lets go
Entirely the West

The Peaks, that lingered last
Remain in Her regret
As scarcely as the Iodine
Upon the Cataract.

*

Banish Air from Air –
Divide Light if you dare –
They'll meet
While Cubes in a Drop
Or Pellets of Shape
Fit
Films cannot annul
Odors return whole
Force Flame
And with a Blonde push
Over your impotence
Flits Steam.

*

As the Starved Maelstrom laps the Navies
As the Vulture teased
Forces the Broods in lonely Valleys
As the Tiger eased

By but a Crumb of Blood, fasts Scarlet
Till he meet a Man
Dainty adorned with Veins and Tissues
And partakes – his Tongue

Cooled by the Morsel for a moment
Grows a fiercer thing
Till he esteem his Dates and Cocoa
A Nutrition mean

I, of a finer Famine
Deem my Supper dry
For but a Berry of Domingo
And a Torrid Eye.

*

I stepped from Plank to Plank
A slow and cautious way
The Stars about my Head I felt
About my Feet the Sea.

I knew not but the next
Would be my final inch –
This gave me that precarious Gait
Some call Experience.

*

Crisis is a Hair
Toward which the forces creep
Past which forces retrograde
If it come in sleep

To suspend the Breath
Is the most we can
Ignorant is it Life or Death
Nicely balancing.

Let an instant push
Or an Atom press
Or a Circle hesitate
In Circumference

It – may jolt the Hand
That adjusts the Hair
That secures Eternity
From presenting – Here –

*

To my quick ear the Leaves – conferred –
The Bushes – they were Bells –
I could not find a Privacy
From Nature's sentinels –

In Cave if I presumed to hide
The Walls – begun to tell –
Creation seemed a mighty Crack –
To make me visible –

*

Of Consciousness, her awful Mate
The Soul cannot be rid –
As easy the secreting her
Behind the Eyes of God.

The deepest hid is sighted first
And scant to Him the Crowd –
What triple Lenses burn upon
The Escapade from God –

*

Fairer through Fading – as the Day
Into the Darkness dips away –
Half Her Complexion of the Sun –
Hindering – Haunting – Perishing –

Rallies Her Glow, like a dying Friend –
Teasing with glittering Amend –
Only to aggravate the Dark
Through an expiring – perfect – look –

*

It is an honorable Thought
And makes One lift One's Hat
As One met sudden Gentlefolk
Upon a daily Street

That We've immortal Place
Though Pyramids decay
And Kingdoms, like the Orchard
Flit Russetly away

*

The Chemical conviction
That Nought be lost
Enable in Disaster
My fractured Trust –

The Faces of the Atoms
If I shall see
How more the Finished Creatures
Departed me!

*

A narrow Fellow in the Grass
Occasionally rides –
You may have met Him – did you not
His notice sudden is –

The Grass divides as with a Comb –
A spotted shaft is seen –
And then it closes at your feet
And opens further on –

He likes a Boggy Acre
A Floor too cool for Corn –
Yet when a Boy, and Barefoot –
I more than once at Noon
Have passed, I thought, a Whip lash
Unbraiding in the Sun
When stooping to secure it
It wrinkled, and was gone –

Several of Nature's People
I know, and they know me –
I feel for them a transport
Of cordiality –

But never met this Fellow
Attended, or alone
Without a tighter breathing
And Zero at the Bone –

*

There is no Silence in the Earth – so silent
As that endured
Which uttered, would discourage Nature
And haunt the World.

*

Further in Summer than the Birds
Pathetic from the Grass
A minor Nation celebrates
Its unobtrusive Mass.

No Ordinance be seen
So gradual the Grace
A pensive Custom it becomes
Enlarging Loneliness.

Antiquest felt at Noon
When August burning low
Arise this spectral Canticle
Repose to typify

Remit as yet no Grace
No Furrow on the Glow
Yet a Druidic Difference
Enhances Nature now

*

The Crickets sang
And set the Sun
And Workmen finished one by one
Their Seam the Day upon.

The low Grass loaded with the Dew
The Twilight stood, as Strangers do
With Hat in Hand, polite and new
To stay as if, or go.

A Vastness, as a Neighbor, came,
A Wisdom, without Face, or Name,
A Peace, as Hemispheres at Home
And so the Night became.

*

Shall I take thee, the Poet said
To the propounded word?
Be stationed with the Candidates
Till I have finer tried –

The Poet searched Philology
And when about to ring
For the suspended Candidate
There came unsummoned in –

That portion of the Vision
The Word applied to fill
Not unto nomination
The Cherubim reveal –

*

The Day grew small, surrounded tight
By early, stooping Night –
The Afternoon in Evening deep
Its Yellow shortness dropt –
The Winds went out their martial ways
The Leaves obtained excuse –
November hung his Granite Hat
Upon a nail of Plush –

*

Great Streets of silence led away
To Neighborhoods of Pause –
Here was no Notice – no Dissent
No Universe – no Laws –

By Clocks, 'twas Morning, and for Night
The Bells at Distance called –
But Epoch had no basis here
For Period exhaled.

*

The Clouds their Backs together laid
The North begun to push
The Forests galloped till they fell
The Lightning played like mice

The Thunder crumbled like a stuff
How good to be in Tombs
Where Nature's Temper cannot reach
Nor missile ever comes

*

The Past is such a curious Creature
To look her in the Face
A Transport may receipt us
Or a Disgrace –

Unarmed if any meet her
I charge him fly
Her faded Ammunition
Might yet reply.

*

A Deed knocks first at Thought
And then – it knocks at Will
That is the manufacturing spot
And Will at Home and well

It then goes out an Act
Or is entombed so still
That only to the ear of God
Its Doom is audible –

*

Like Rain it sounded till it curved
And then I knew 'twas Wind –
It walked as wet as any Wave
But swept as dry as sand –
When it had pushed itself away
To some remotest Plain
A coming as of Hosts was heard
That was indeed the Rain –
It filled the Wells, it pleased the Pools
It warbled in the Road –
It pulled the spigot from the Hills
And let the Floods abroad, –
It loosened acres, lifted seas
The sites of Centres stirred
Then like Elijah rode away
Upon a Wheel of Cloud.

*

To flee from memory
Had we the Wings
Many would fly
Inured to slower things
Birds with surprise
Would scan the cowering Van
Of men escaping
From mind of man

*

The Butterfly in honored Dust
Assuredly will lie
But none will pass the Catacomb
So chastened as the Fly –

*

To pile like Thunder to its close
Then crumble grand away
While Everything created hid
This – would be Poetry –

Or Love – the two coeval come –
We both and neither prove –
Experience either and consume –
For None see God and live –

*

A Wind that rose
Though not a Leaf
In any Forest stirred
But with itself did cold engage
Beyond the Realm of Bird –
A Wind that woke a lone Delight
Like Separation's Swell
Restored in Arctic Confidence
To the Invisible –

*

I think that the Root of the Wind is Water –
It would not sound so deep
Were it a Firmamental Product –
Airs no Ocean keep –
Mediterranean intonations –
To a Current's Ear –
There is a maritime conviction
In the Atmosphere –

*

It sounded as if the Streets were running
And then – the Streets stood still –
Eclipse – was all we could see at the Window
And Awe – was all we could feel.

By and by – the boldest stole out of his Covert
To see if Time was there –
Nature was in an Opal Apron,
Mixing fresher Air.

*

Could mortal lip divine
The undeveloped Freight
Of a delivered syllable
'Twould crumble with the weight.

*

A Route of Evanescence
With a revolving Wheel –
A Resonance of Emerald –
A Rush of Cochineal –
And every Blossom on the Bush
Adjusts its tumbled Head –
The mail from Tunis, probably,
An easy Morning's Ride –

*

How happy is the little Stone
That rambles in the Road alone,
And doesn't care about Careers
And Exigencies never fears –
Whose Coat of elemental Brown
A passing Universe put on,
And independent as the Sun
Associates or glows alone,
Fulfilling absolute Decree
In casual simplicity –

*

The Life that tied too tight escapes
Will ever after run
With a prudential look behind
And spectres of the Rein –
The Horse that scents the living Grass
And sees the Pastures smile,
Will be retaken with a shot
If he is caught at all –

*

As imperceptibly as Grief
The Summer lapsed away –
Too imperceptible at last
To seem like Perfidy –
A Quietness distilled
As Twilight long begun,
Or Nature spending with herself
Sequestered Afternoon –
The Dusk drew earlier in –
The Morning foreign shone –
A courteous, yet harrowing Grace,
As Guest, that would be gone –
And thus, without a Wing
Or service of a Keel
Our Summer made her light escape
Into the Beautiful.

*

Those – dying then,
Knew where they went –
They went to God's Right Hand
That Hand is amputated now
And God cannot be found –

The abdication of Belief
Makes the Behavior small –
Better an ignis fatuus
Than no illume at all –

*

How slow the Wind –
how slow the sea –
how late their Feathers be!

*

There came a Wind like a Bugle –
It quivered through the Grass
And a Green Chill upon the Heat
So ominous did pass
We barred the Windows and the Doors
As from an Emerald Ghost –
The Doom's electric Moccasin
That very instant passed –
On a strange Mob of panting Trees
And Fences fled away
And Rivers where the Houses ran
Those looked that lived – that Day –
The Bell within the steeple wild
The flying tidings told –
How much can come
And much can go,
And yet abide the World!

*

By homely gift and hindered Words
The human heart is told
Of Nothing –
'Nothing' is the force
That renovates the World –

*

A World made penniless by that departure
Of minor fabrics begs
But sustenance is of the spirit
The Gods but Dregs

*

A Drunkard cannot meet a Cork
Without a Revery –
And so encountering a Fly
This January Day
Jamaicas of Remembrance stir
That send me reeling in –
The moderate drinker of Delight
Does not deserve the spring –
Of juleps, part are in the Jug
And more are in the joy –
Your connoisseur in Liquors
Consults the Bumble Bee –

*

The right to perish might be thought
An undisputed right –
Attempt it, and the Universe
Upon the opposite
Will concentrate its officers –
You cannot even die
But nature and mankind must pause
To pay you scrutiny.

*

A face devoid of love or grace,
A hateful, hard, successful face,
A face with which a stone
Would feel as thoroughly at ease
As were they old acquaintances –
First time together thrown.

*

Did life's penurious length
Italicize its sweetness,
The men that daily live
Would stand so deep in joy
That it would clog the cogs
Of that revolving reason
Whose esoteric belt
Protects our sanity.

*

Drowning is not so pitiful
As the attempt to rise.
Three times, 'tis said, a sinking man
Comes up to face the skies,
And then declines forever
To that abhorred abode,
Where hope and he part company –
For he is grasped of God.
The Maker's cordial visage,
However good to see,
Is shunned, we must admit it,
Like an adversity.

*

Love can do all but raise the Dead
I doubt if even that
From such a giant were withheld
Were flesh equivalent

But love is tired and must sleep,
And hungry and must graze
And so abets the shining Fleet
Till it is out of gaze.

*

The waters chased him as he fled,
Not daring look behind –
A billow whispered in his Ear,
'Come home with me, my friend –

My parlor is of shriven glass,
My pantry has a fish
For every palate in the Year' –
To this revolting bliss
The object floating at his side
Made no distinct reply.

*

The reticent volcano keeps
His never slumbering plan –
Confided are his projects pink
To no precarious man.

If nature will not tell the tale
Jehovah told to her
Can human nature not survive
Without a listener?

Admonished by her buckled lips
Let every babbler be
The only secret people keep
Is Immortality.

*

Experiment escorts us last –
His pungent company
Will not allow an Axiom
An Opportunity